IT'S YOUR DECISION

Make it NOW!

A Back to Basics Handbook on Life's Everyday Choices

By
Sharath Shanth

The publisher and the author do not make any guarantee
or other promise as to any results that may be obtained
from using the content of this book. To the maximum extent
permitted by law, the publisher and the author disclaim all
liability in the event any information, commentary, analysis,
opinions, advice and/or recommendations contained in this
book prove to be inaccurate, incomplete or unreliable, or
result in any investment or other losses.

It's Your Decision
Copyright © 2021 Sharath Shanth

TABLE OF CONTENTS

PREFACE

The Coronavirus has been a global pandemic, and it has touched all our lives in so many ways. It has changed man's view of nature's effect on humanity and helped us realise how interconnected the world's populations are with each other.

So, it's important to acknowledge this as an opportunity to grow and not take any decision we make in life too lightly, no matter how small.

Yet, out of this dark period came a new understanding by many:
- We understand how not to take our lives for granted.
- We understand how to value our friends.
- We understand the people who care and those who don't.
- We understand we often waste time with negative and toxic people.
- We understand the value of exercising and how to do it with discipline.
- We understand that filling our minds with worthless information can cause us to be moody and pessimistic.
- We understand that time is not always on our side. It continues irrespective of our wishes. Therefore, it is on us to make the most of it.
- We understand to be comfortable in our own skin. All we own in this life are our minds and bodies. It's up to us to take care of them and make the most of them.

- We understand to never run after money, as money never runs after you.
- We understand why we should help people yet determine the amount of help within our capabilities.
- We understand that excessive spending is not required to live within our means. Being frugal is not negative.
- We understand the world will never be the same again, in how we interact with care for our hygiene and our civic sense to society.

I hope everyone understands to value our lives; we should be the best judge on how we live our lives, do things consciously and learn to say NO, and most of all…Stay Safe!

Just as we have learned to live more safely in this new pandemic age, take some time to look at other ways we can live better lives. It can be as simple as choosing the right beverage or buying life insurance. It's Your Decision will explore eighteen everyday aspects of our daily lives where we can make better, healthier, and more profitable choices.

CHAPTER 1
The Importance of Now

There is never a more critical time in your life than NOW. But, unfortunately, so many people delay deciding to take steps to change their lives; they make excuses and reasons why they would fail and don't make the next move.

I'm often reminded of Scarlett O'Hara's famous line from *Gone with the Wind*, "I won't think about that now; I'll think about it tomorrow." Unfortunately, so many people take that approach to the simplest decisions they make in their daily lives. Whether it's a diet they have been considering or acting on a new business idea, people often fear failure and decide that "tomorrow" will be a better day to start.

There will never be a more appropriate time to take the next step than the point you are at NOW. So, take the steps needed to get ready to take control of your life.

For example, when you decide to create a start-up business but don't have enough money to go ahead with it, don't forget the dream; take the steps necessary to achieve it:

- Start saving money
- Start developing your business plan.
- Start determining possible ways to finance it.
- Start creating your marketing plan, so you are ready to begin from day one.

There is never a point where you can know it all; there will always be a learning curve. But this shouldn't stop you from moving forward. You can learn as you go. If this is your first venture, just remember, you are not ever too young to start something, Mark Zuckerberg started Facebook at 20, Steve Jobs started Apple at 21, Jeff Bezos started Amazon at 30, and Bill Gates started Microsoft at 32. These are just a few people who took their ideas to completion by not giving up. The younger you are, the more risk you can take when starting a business, as you have time in your favour. Everything takes time; if you start a business in your 20's versus in your 50's you still need time to help the company grow, so the earlier, the better. But these entrepreneurs also knew that success wouldn't happen overnight. Even in the most prosperous gardens, a mango tree starts as a tiny seed that takes 5 to 8 years to bear fruit. And likewise, it takes time for a business to grow and prosper. So, be persistent AND patient, and one day your business will bear its delicious fruit.

Likewise, you are never too old to start a new dream.

Colonel Sanders started KFC at age 40, Bernie Marcus co-founded Home Depot at 50, Charles Ranlett Flint launched IBM at 61, and Bob Parsons started GoDaddy at 47.

What is important is your drive, not your age. You must channel your ambitions in the right direction and put in the hours and hard work. One day it will pay off, but the importance is the time and effort you put towards it. Even if your endeavour does not succeed the first time, its failure can be a bridge to your ultimate success.

Although we have been discussing starting a new business, the importance of NOW is ever-present in our lives. I have created nine companies from the ground up, and I ask the same questions no matter what challenge lies ahead of me. Whether it is a relationship, continuing your education, or creating a new physical "you", these challenges all require the same dedication, persistence and patience.

Never complain about the odds not being in your favour – if you want to complain that the universe is not in sync with you, one can write a book together on excuses; the list is endless.

Have your priorities in line – always determine what is most important to you and what has to get done immediately. Nobody can plan this for you; you must master it yourself and make it on your own. If you get help along the way, great. But overall, it is your journey, and you must take matters into your own hands.

Sacrifice – learn to see the big picture. If you want to reach the top, you cannot expect to get there without a few sacrifices along the way. Some will be good for you, and some may be painful, but always look at the big picture and then decide what is worth sacrificing to make it happen.

The power of positivity – believe in yourself, be positive and remain positive. Then, keep saying it till it sinks into your subconscious, and you believe it, keep saying it till it becomes a habit, and habits will lead to change and create results.

You will hit a few road bumps on the road to success, and that's fine; it's not going to be easy sailing the whole journey. The road bumps discourage the weak from moving forward; you must learn to leap over them (without bottoming out) and move forward.

In business terms, we call it barriers of entry. Businesses make their roads complex and complicated to avoid competitors from entering their space. These can include high start-up costs, regulatory hurdles, or other obstacles preventing new competitors from entering a business sector easily. It is a practice even taught at business school. So, it is normal to have these bumps in your journey; just remember not to lose faith and keep your eye on the prize.

Believe in yourself; you are an agent of change. Every person in the world has an impact, whether you want it or not. For example, when someone first told me to recycle, I resisted. I knew other people did it, but why should I get into it?. However, as I grew older, I realised that if more people thought like me, it would be catastrophic to our environment. So, I started to recycle. Every time I did, it would make a difference because my neighbour saw me recycling and eventually did so themselves. It becomes a chain reaction. Now you have two people recycling, and they encourage two more, and it continues to multiply until it has a tremendous impact on the health of our planet.

Everybody has ideas and dreams,
but only a few can convert them into Reality.
Wake up today; the time is NOW.

CHAPTER 2
Lessons For You and To Share with Others

Here are a few valuable everyday lessons to cultivate and use to help in your daily journey through life. Embracing these fundamental principles will help you develop the steps needed for NOW and grow to your full potential.

Keep a diary -- a diary records your thoughts at a particular time and helps you plan for the future by keeping a journal of your past experiences. Then, you can look back at it and see how you progressed and the steps you took to get there. Many people make mistakes in keeping a diary; they push themselves to write every day, which is not necessary for it to be helpful. Instead, consider it as creating your life's blueprint, which you can update from time to time to acknowledge your accomplishments and what remains on your "bucket list". If you don't want to call it a diary, make your diary a "to-do list" and use it as a great motivational tool.

Ask -- many people tend to be overconfident and not ask for help. If they don't understand something, they don't want to be the stupid one in the room, so they remain silent. The power of asking teaches you the importance of eliminating miscommunication and misunderstanding. Remember, "if you don't ask the question, the answer is always NO."

Help others -- there is an ultimate joy when you help someone. My mother always told me, "when you can help, you should help". It doesn't have to be a grand gesture or something beyond your means. It could be just lending a hand to someone at the airport or helping someone figure something out. Help is not always about money. Many people cannot help financially, but they can help in other ways, often proving much more valuable than money. Having a shoulder to cry on or getting a hug can sometimes save someone's life. Always be willing to help if you can; you will be making the world a better place by being humble and selfless.

Elderly advice -- always listen to your elders, you don't have to agree with their way of thinking, but you can definitely learn something from them. It's simple logic; they have experienced life more than you, so getting a few pointers is never a bad thing. Listen to them and store that information away. It may come in handy and help you one day.

How to hold your tongue -- when you are having a discussion or an argument, and the other party is stubborn, you need to be patient and not go head to head with the other person. They probably won't even listen to what you are saying. Instead, be patient, wait for them to finish, calm down, and then state your case. If you still disagree, understand that they don't have to agree with you. There isn't a prize, and we are all entitled to have a different opinion. It is beneficial to have different views; that's why governments have left-wing and right-wing political parties. Just make sure that you don't take their opinion personally or make them feel they are wrong with any discussion or argument. Rather, you can tell them why you think the way you do and let them understand why. They might even give you a reason to change your opinion.

Be confident in your identity -- never be ashamed about where you came from, such as a small, rural town or a low-income family. Whenever you feel like this, remember that your background brought you to where you are today, which in many cases would have been unimaginable to you as a child. If you feel uncomfortable where you are, it is because you don't feel you belong there. Societal norms and classifications of people exacerbate this way of thinking. You must understand you have the same number of fingers, eyes and nose as everybody else. Also, Bill Gates and you have the same number of hours in a day. It is up to you to determine what you do with your time and decide where life takes you. If anyone tries to put you down, it is merely a test, and how you handle the situation determines the outcome.

Life doesn't always give you lemons – we've all heard the expression "when life gives you lemons, make lemonade"; well, what if you don't like lemons? In life, opportunities are always present, and you decide which interests you and those that don't. You will have many choices to make in life, which we call the "opportunity cost" in the business world. When we choose, we give up another option we could have taken at that time. So, you must decide whether it is worth it or not.

For some, going to university or starting to work is a choice they must make. Many college dropouts have achieved everything they wanted in life. Everyone is unique, so don't compare yourself with another to measure your success. You may be on the same journey, but you are not in the same boat as them. In high school, I had friends who would only need to study for an hour and excel in their grades.

Yet, I had to spend hours or even days prepping to get the same grade. In the end, nobody cares about how much time you have invested in it, only the end result. So, we must focus on the destination and understand that we all have different roads to get there, but our goal is the same: to reach our destination. You can apply this to almost every walk of life; a skilled carpenter might take an hour to repair a table. Someone without that level of skill might take hours or even days to struggle to do it. But in the end, we need it fixed, and that's what matters. So, don't blame the struggle; everyone has their battles to face to achieve victory. Life isn't the same for everyone; nobody chooses to be born into the lives they lead.

Is education important? -- Some believe that education will help you get a job or go through life with flying colours; I'm sorry to burst your bubble, but it isn't the case. One must look at education as brain food; it broadens your mind to show you the possibilities and places that might interest you. Studying the past often gives you guidance for the future. People sometimes get frustrated in high school, thinking, "why do we need to learn something that we will never use" but in reality, it is a brain exercise. It helps the students know if they might want to pursue this field of study. Everything you learn in school (and remember) will probably come in handy one day. At the very least, you may be able to help your children when they are studying the same subject in school. Education is the tool for determining your future interests and how to use this knowledge to achieve them.

Never give up on your goal -- this is easier said than done. The key to achieving your goal is persistence. For any goal we have, there should be an earnest desire to achieve it. If you build a road map towards it and determine the steps you must take to reach it, you will encounter crossroads and detours like every journey. You must make the necessary choices to move further, and if you fall into a ditch, you must understand you put yourself in there, so only you have the power to get out.

Once you are on your journey, you will face moments of doubt, whether this was the right choice to make or chasing the right dream. The decisions you make are your decisions, and you should know you have to stand by that decision, so be focused on learning what choice you have to make.

It's okay to switch to another road, but it should be to reach the same goal. The difference between a winner and a loser is that one gets to the finish line, and the other doesn't. The game, however, is not played with anyone but yourself, and it ends with you.

Always believe in yourself

"The truth will only have one straightforward answer; the lies are the ones that will have different variations" – Mani

CHAPTER 3
Taking Advice from a Five-Year-Old
Awakening Your Inner Child

A five-year-old makes decisions based on simple truths of what he needs and what he has been taught about how to get what he needs. A five-year-old is all about NOW. He wants to be fed, get new toys, and receive the loving care of his parents. And he quickly learns the truth about how to get what he wants. Unfortunately, as we grow older, we get blinded by our everyday life, information flooding in the news media, and the people we interact with daily. As a result, we tend to forget the truth of the situation and how to achieve our needs most effectively.

"Children are our greatest treasure; they are our future."
… Nelson Mandela

It is the truth of the situation; they are the future, so how they are raised and educated will determine how successful the next generation will be. All our advancements in our world today were the dreams of children who have grown up.

Many solutions begin in a five-year-old's mind. For example, when we would ask the boy or girl, "what do you want to do," they would say, "I want to go to the moon," or if you ask a child playing with legos, "what are you trying to build," they reply, "the biggest building in the world" and the list goes. Today, we are sending spaceships to mars and have the tallest building built at 868 meters. Never underestimate the power of a child's imagination.

In life, we sometimes get told, "be realistic" and shelve our dreams, often because nobody believes in it, or others think it's impossible. The truth is the five-year-old's dream is not an impossible dream; it's a vision that will require much work to achieve. For example, to reach the moon, the dream began in the 18th century (or before) but only became possible in the 1960s. The same goes for the predictions of Socrates and Leonardo da Vinci. The vision is often realistic, but one needs time and technical advancement to bring that vision to reality.

When we have problems or are in a challenging situation, we seldom seek advice from the young five-year-old. We think that they wouldn't understand or how can they even relate, yet at the same time, they have the purest form of information and are more intelligent than we can even realise.

As we grow into our teenage years, we don't understand the value of our childhood. As teenagers, we learn how to think but don't always assimilate our life's experiences up to that point.

But, once you reach your mid 20's, you begin to awaken and remember those parts of your childhood that moulded us into the person you became.

And eventually, our adulthood can go in two directions. It either tries to diminish our inner child's dreams with a dose of reality or listens to the inner child to achieve new dreams and ambitions gathered over the years.

When we look at ourselves in the mirror, we can always find the five-year-old in us, or any other year no matter how old we have become.

The beginning years are always important not only for an individual but also for a business and anything that grows. So, always consider your life's journey as the life of the tree. When a seed is first put in the soil to grow, it will first form into a tiny sapling. At this stage, it is very fragile, like a child or any start-up for that matter. However, as you nurture and protect it, it gets stronger, and with time and the proper care, it will turn into a strong tree able to resist the elements. This is also the fate of a child growing into an adult. Given the right care and nutrients, with time, the child will grow strong and resilient, and the same goes for a business as well.
If you are a parent or an elder sibling, always remember to help the younger generation grow stronger to help them achieve their potential.

CHAPTER 4
Becoming a Better Parent

The choices we make as a parent can have an immense effect on our children and even the world. When we teach our children to live in the NOW and make decisions based on truth and not fear, then we open a window to a limitless world to them.

There are a tremendous number of books on parenting and how to raise your kid, from books to tutorial videos to YouTube videos, even podcasts for that matter. This chapter will highlight certain behaviours often found in children and discuss how to correct them. Remember that we are all human and make mistakes; this is normal but understanding our mistakes and correcting them is a big step.

Everyone feels they are the best at what they do, and they probably are for the most part, but there is always room to improve and learn.

Young children are like a sponge. They absorb what they are exposed to, and they start processing this information sooner than you think. It moulds them into the person they will become, so it's essential that you point them in the right direction. It is the time and place in their life when they should learn about choices and the pitfalls of making the wrong ones.

Being rude – if a child behaves rudely, they have learned it from their parents' attitude or others around them. Everyone in the house must understand that the child is a sponge and the adults' behaviour directly affects them. Therefore, they will tend to mimic this behaviour because they think it is okay to behave like this in the outside world if it seems acceptable in their home.

Lying – a major reason kids lie is that when they had made a mistake in the past, their parents overreacted, causing the child to be afraid to tell the truth, the next time. The child thinks, "If I lie and my parents don't find out, I can get away with it." Or they might think, "I don't want to worry them." Then, the reason for the lie starts evolving into a more reasonable decision. One must understand, we all make mistakes, and if your child, even as a teenager, lies and you find out it's a lie, control your emotions and deal with it as a real-life situation together. The child will more likely confide in their parents if they feel safe doing so.

Running an army schedule – many parents want their kids to behave appropriately and achieve everything, sometimes more than they can accomplish. But when you start treating your children like soldiers and order them around, they begin to lose empathy for others. They will not care about understanding other people's feelings because they think their parents don't care about their feelings.

It works in the army as well. There is a saying when you join up, they first break you and then they build you into a soldier. Being a soldier leaves no room for emotion as they train you to be a machine. So, when many come back to society, they find it challenging to deal with emotions and respect people's feelings, even those who care the most.

Also, whenever you discipline your child, NEVER do it in public, even in front of their siblings or relatives. No matter how close you are to them, your child doesn't know that, and they will feel broken inside. It eventually will cause the child to never stand up for themselves and possibly needing therapy in their 30's for their lack of self-esteem.

Smothering (overprotective) - parents sometimes tend to smother their child with love and affection, especially if it is their only or first child. It may seem very cute and caring, but it doesn't teach their children to face obstacles and challenges in their lives by doing this. Your child can become a coward. They will have to fight their own battles at an older age eventually. This fear makes it embarrassing or even harder for the simplest obstacles life has to offer.

Always encourage your child to learn the basic skills they need like cooking, laundry and cleaning, no matter how affluent and wealthy you are. Don't deny your children learning these; it will help them relate to others and even make friends by talking about how much they hate their chores.

If your child has low self-esteem or is not confident, it could be because you make all their decisions rather than encourage them to make their own. Take a close look at your parenting skills and determine what you thought was valuable and what wasn't; yet keep in mind your child might have a completely different dream from yours.

Encourage your children to make choices rather than smothering them by offering them everything. For example, make them decide what they want to eat, and even if you're going to buy them a present, ask them what they want from the choices you give them. Giving them a choice will help them learn they have to decide on things. If they choose the wrong one, they must learn to accept their decision. Such is the art of decision making.

Misbehaviour – I often see kids that are destructive and mean, and I wonder why. It sometimes stems from when they are well behaved, and nobody seems to notice or acknowledge their good behaviour. But when they misbehave, they get attention. This call for attention roots down to a toddler. When they start crying, their parents pay attention to them, so they consistently cry to get their attention.

However, if you keep talking and interacting with the child when it behaves well, they will learn that good behaviour gets the attention they want and much more pleasurable attention at that. Don't get so caught up in your everyday life that you ignore the joy of having your child. And let them know that.

Understanding Your Parents - As children, we often believe our parents are superheroes and the wisest of all. But, more than anything, we expect them to read our minds and know what we want and think. I'm discussing this with you, an adult, because understanding our parents is a lifelong endeavour, even after they have passed from this earth.

As we become adults, it is helpful to look back at our parents and know that they hadn't a clue how to raise children. They didn't go to a training school on how to become a parent. Most parents have had no prior experience in raising a child. So, if you are a firstborn, you must realise they are doing everything for the first time. Although they are new to this, the same way you suck at playing a video game the first time, they will get better over time.

If you think they will get it right the second time, well, they haven't handled two children at once, but know one thing: every parent is trying their best to make it right for you.

Parents want their kids to achieve everything they haven't, so they always push their kids to get more out of life, or else they feel they haven't done their best as a parent. Know that they have sacrificed the time and effort in their life to take care of you and for you to achieve your goals. It may seem suffocating and overwhelming, but remember, it comes from a good place.

CHAPTER 5
What To Drink When Travelling

You may ask, "Why put this in the book?"

Life's challenges usually are a matter of making a choice. Although we generally have to tackle more complicated issues, many make basic choices without much thought. But, unfortunately, if we don't live in the NOW, we often make decisions based on our habits, often bad ones.

Water is nature's gift to man, but it can be your worst enemy when travelling. In the west, people drink water from the tap or filtered water and get accustomed to it. However, when they travel, the change of alkalinity and composition content can cause people to become sick because of the change in environment.

Our immune systems adapt to where we live. We are used to a particular composition in our water. People tend to feel safe when consuming bottled water. However, even these can have elements foreign to our bodies since they come from different regions.

Today, bottled water choices include packaged drinking, distilled water, mineral water, and then the list goes on with speciality water such as artisanal water, volcanic water, etc.

The health issues in unregulated or third-world countries occur when the companies adulterate or repackage it, mainly by tampering with the bottle, refilling it with other water, and resealing it.

In my experience over the years where I have fallen sick in Egypt, Italy, India, Thailand, and many other places, I now realise the best way to be safe is to drink sparkling water. It is difficult to tamper with it since the bubbles and gas escape, causing the water to be flat. So, you will know if it has been tampered with, and besides that, sparkling water fills you up, so you won't overeat while travelling.

For many, the obvious choice is coke/sprite or any international carbonated drink where it would be safe as a multinational corporation would never compromise on their quality.

But then again, these are filled with tons of sugar. However, if you choose a carbonated drink, be sure to have it cold but avoid ice. Cold sparkling water is the best choice, with lime and no ice. And if it's the small sparkling bottle, stick a lime wedge it in, as we do with our beer.

CHAPTER 6
Surviving a Hangover

If you didn't read Chapter 5, this could be the result. Hangovers are as prevalent as the common cold, to such an extent that even medical and refreshment companies have started targeting this segment of the population.

Here are our ways to handle a hangover like a champion:
If you know you are going to have (or have had) a heavy drinking session, here are some tips for mitigating a hangover that you can do NOW if you plan on drinking:

1. Eat lentil soup before your drink. It coats the lining of your stomach, preventing stomach acids from irritating your lining.
2. Eat boiled eggs or meats, which are high in protein. They help line the stomach as well.
3. Drink buttermilk a couple of hours before you start drinking; it lines the stomach as well and protects it from irritation.
4. Avoid Indian food or spicy food before drinking or while drinking. Eating these foods generally loosen the muscles in your stomach, and drinking alcohol further aggravates it. It even can cause you to throw up and most definitely have heartburn the next day. If you reach that point, the best way to tackle that is to have a glass of cold milk, buttermilk, or take some Pepto Bismol.

5. Try to avoid drinks with sugary mixers, as the sweeter the beverage, the greater the hangover. Instead, have "neat" spirits on ice, wine or beer; it helps avoid a hangover.

6. Rule of thumb, the darker the drink, the darker the hangover.

7. Stick to 1 type of alcohol the whole night, don't mix your types of alcohol. Mixing would be like putting a red carpet out for the hangover; the less you mix, the better.

8. While drinking, have breaks in between and keep hydrating along the way, preferably with sparkling water; they work wonders.

9. Take effervescent tablets at the end of the night (the regular over the counter vitamin tablets).

10. Take a mild paracetamol at the end of your night (caution: consult your doctor if you're allergic), but if you are used to taking them, have a regular dose of 1 or 2.

11. Drink a litre of water before going to bed to avoid headaches in the morning. Alcohol dehydrates you, causing the headache; so, hydration is key

Remedies so you won't behave like a zombie:

1. For champions, you can recover from a hangover with a "hair of the dog", either a beer or Bloody Mary.

2. If you don't want to drink the next day, scrambled eggs are the best option. Eggs have vitamin B and zinc, which help in tackling the alcohol in your body.

3. Load up on the carbs to absorb all the alcohol. We all know bread expands when consumed and is terrible when you're on a diet, but when recovering from a hangover, bread can be your best friend.

4. Guacamole will make you happy and feel better. But, of course, it goes well with a Bloody Mary too.

5. Fruits and vegetables with high water content help recovery, so apples, watermelon, and cucumbers are excellent choices.

6. When you drink too much, your body will want something unhealthy like fried foods. You won't be able to finish it, I assure you. Even though you think you are hungry and have major cravings, you will have a major loss of appetite. It's your mind playing games with you. Don't be fooled.

7. Coconut water is the best electrolyte and does wonders for a hangover.

8. Get in a workout; You will sweat out the toxins.

The principal cure for a hangover is hydrating and getting the alcohol out of your body. The way to do this is to flush out the toxins by drinking water and juices or eating and having the alcohol absorbed and digested faster. This way, you can get it out of the system and get on with your day.

CHAPTER 7
Surviving a Break-up

A break-up can be challenging to handle. Yet, this is the decision that most find one of the most difficult in their lives. It is certainly something that we don't want to make NOW, but the choice is often there, and we must deal with it, utilising all the strengths we have learned in our lives.

Everyone has their threshold when it comes to pain. A relationship can be overwhelming at the start. During the first six months (the honeymoon phase), you discover your other half's faults and habits, the good and the bad, and make them a part of your daily life schedule.

Even if you don't meet them every day, you usually speak with them, chat with them, or communicate with them in one form or another.

This communication turns into a routine and becomes a habit, and when you break up, it is a habit that's hard to break.

Usually, the two situations you end up being in is either:

If you are the one getting dumped, you feel rejected, and you think you are the cause of the break-up, irrespective of whose fault it is.

To get over it, you need to understand what evolved to change the relationship and not who was at fault, which technically is closure. It sometimes takes a while for one to comprehend this. You start questioning your behaviour and begin thinking in terms of cause and effect. It can put you on edge as you expect this to happen again, and you will always doubt the other person.

If you are the "dumpee", you will be happy at first that it is over, as the relationship was painful, but after a period, a void will start kicking in, and then you might start questioning whether you made the right decision and if it was worth it. Then, one rationalises the relationship in positive terms and make excuses for the negative situations. Finally, you might start wanting the relationship back; you'd rather be in a miserable relationship than be alone. So, even if your partner has moved on, you hold onto the image of wanting it back.

People tend to forget that nothing in life is permanent, not even life itself, and everyone you meet in life impacts your life one way or the other. I always believe there are two kinds of people in life that you will encounter,
1. The people who put life into you
2. The people who take life out of you

You will always have both kinds; sometimes, the people who take life out of you end up being family members or people in your daily routine. The only way you can attain balance is to surround yourself with more people who put life into you and fewer people who take it out of you. It makes life more bearable and you, in turn, create a support system that will help deal with situations when the ones who take life out of you fill you up with negativity.

At times the person in your relationship is the one that is taking life out of you. So, the answer is to get away from the relationship, which you can make happen. But at times, it's easier said than done, hence why you must end it so you can make it through

.

A break-up varies in magnitude with the number of years and the amount of time you put in a relationship. The longer it is, the greater the impact. One tends to hold on to the memories (good and bad), which can get very complicated. The weight of the memories is also why some relationships are successful because it is the same reason people stay together.

It is important to start looking at it from how you usually spend your day and begin working to adapt that to being single and how it will help you move forward in what decisions you want to make for the future.

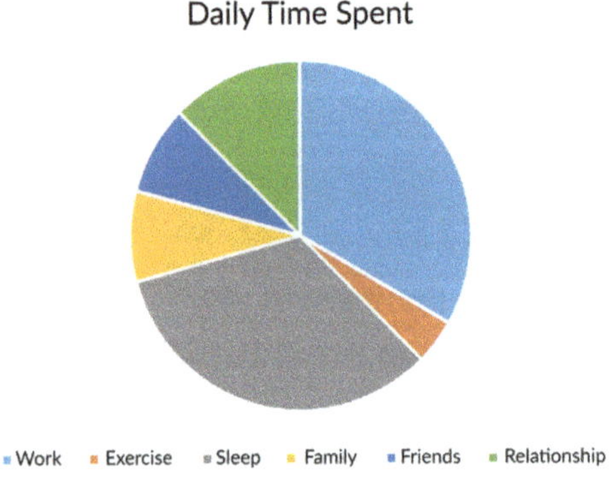

Work	8
Exercise	1
Sleep	8
Family	2
Friends	2
Relationship	3

This chart shows you roughly how you might spend 24 hours in your day. Of course, these time equations vary depending on the person and occupation. The reason to depict it as a pie chart is to help one understand when you go through a break-up (either being dumped or being the dumpee), you eliminate the relationship slice.

And now there is a void, in this case, an extra three hours. You must fill these hours, either by extending the time spent on other things or finding a new activity or hobby to replace them. If you don't, you feel a void. Then you start questioning if it was the right decision. Instead, you should find something positive to do to fill up the time, such as beginning a new hobby, learning a new language or skill, or starting a new workout program to get you primed for the singles market. It is important to do something positive that will impact your life and make you proud. Don't just let the void sit there and think time itself will heal it. You are in control if you just choose to do so.

Taking control of your situation is key in dealing with a break-up, one day at a time.

CHAPTER 8
Stereotyping and Racism are the Same Things

When we meet someone, we assume we understand their behaviour and culture from past experiences with the same nationality or what we have heard about their "kind" of people. Just as a young child makes decisions based on what they have learned about people, as adults, we "categorise" people by our perspective about their culture. NOW is NOT the time to fall unconsciously into that precipice of stereotyping people we don't know.

For example, in the Middle East, we mainly find Filipinos in the service sector like fast-food chains, clerical jobs and so forth. You won't find many of them as business owners or managers of corporations in the region. So, people in the Middle East always look down on them as a lower race.

However, this isn't true. For example, in the Philippines, there are many qualified scientists, doctors, pilots, ministers and many professions. But, because of those found in the Middle East, their race in the Middle East will only know them as common labourers because of their jobs.

The same is true for the Saudis in America; their stereotype is that everyone is either a prince or is extremely well off. However, if you go to the kingdom of Saudi Arabia, you see people working in jobs through the whole employment spectrum and trying to make a living just like everyone else.

Indians in the Middle East can be common labourers or the wealthiest billionaires in the country. However, most stereotype them as migrant lower-class workers. On the other hand, in America, most Indians are professors, doctors, scientists, etc. Therefore, they stereotype them as either being good with money or super smart, which is totally different from the popular opinion of the Middle East.

As the world's population becomes more mobile, many people from foreign countries seek their fortune in other lands. However, the home country residents often view this migration negatively because they view them as usurpers of their land's fortunes.

Racism had its early beginnings with slavery in the United States and continues today with all people of colour.

The other reason you find large quantities of people of another race in a foreign country is that they migrated there, either because they were previously colonised or because of other calamities and revolutions. For example, the Iranian revolution displaced many Persians to America and other parts of Europe.

When these people migrated, the locals had made their stereotypical view of them, often fostered by the movies or what they had heard about them. They saw these people in such a one dimensional way that they didn't even want to get to know them as they really were.

This is not true. In the same culture, you wouldn't consider yourself and the person next to you of the same background to be the same, so why would you think someone from another race is just like everyone else in their race.

If we were all the same, we would all have the same needs and wants. So, the easiest way to wrap your head around the idea is that we are all uniquely common. Of course, we are all unique individuals, but when you put us all together, we create a society with similarities amongst its members, yet individually we are different.

One tends to forget that every person is unique and put them in the box of their perception of the race. As a result, people often think they all behave the same way as if they are all cut from the same cloth.

However, people from all backgrounds have been breaking barriers and stereotypes, so it's almost impossible to judge anyone anymore (not that you should) to say one race is more powerful than the other.

The best way to avoid stereotyping and racism is by learning about different cultures -- their history, needs, traditions, and customs. It will help you when you wonder why they sometimes act differently than you do.

Just as we all have different needs, different cultures have customs that might seem foreign to us. That doesn't make them odd or backward; it is quite common in their homeland. In some countries, handshakes and greetings in cultures are done in a manner you might not understand. In Arabic, some think "As-Salaam-Alaikum" means "hello" or "how are you", but it actually means "peace be upon you". When Indian Hindus touch their elders' feet, it's not to bow down to a person, but to respect their experience and knowledge as the elder has walked through life more than you, hence the gesture.

CHAPTER 9
Shine: The Power of the First Impression

The first impression is often the last impression we have of someone – we begin to build our opinion on what we see and hear the first time we meet them. If it were a business meeting and a person walks into your office with shorts and a flip flop, nobody is going to take him seriously.

The same goes if you are meeting someone on a first date. If your date (or you) is poorly dressed, it is doubtful that the date will go well. It appears the poorly dressed person is not taking the date seriously or doesn't think it's worth the effort.

Too often, people decide to try to "size-up" a person before fully revealing themselves to them. Unfortunately, this fear of not embracing the NOW in the first meeting often results in less than encouraging results.

The impact of the first impression, however, actually depends on the type of person. People can be introverts and extroverts. Extroverts are more confident and comfortable expressing themselves. What they lack in lustre can make up for it in their speech, and what they put on the table, i.e., actions speak louder than words.

But if you're an introvert, you are more into listening than expressing yourself at the first meeting. Others need to make an effort and take the time to get to know you. They may or may not choose to do so.

Businesses and organisations must value and nurture their first impression. Otherwise, the business will not attract new customers. Unfortunately, this is where many long-standing companies drop the ball. They take their existing customers for granted and lose sight of making a good first impression on new ones. Nobody would deliberately choose a disorganised company for their business needs.

The important thing for everyone to consider is not simply the first impression, as everyone is different in their acceptance of information. Instead, the lasting impression is what makes all the difference.

We often assume that materialistic wealth and a life of luxury is what we want to achieve. Our goals, in general, are for happiness, health and peace of mind. However, in the rat race, we get blinded and define a person by their wealth and luxurious lifestyle. A person driving a Mercedes Benz instantly creates a first impression of success, whether true or not.

Knowing this, we should turn it to our advantage and look at ourselves from a third person's point of view. Modifying how we dress or what we choose to speak about will help you capitalise on your impression in a conversation, meeting, or that special date you want to impress.

I used to wear a suit every day to work until a friend in New York told me a story. He said that if you took your car to a garage to get it fixed and the mechanic was formally dressed, you would think either this place is too expensive or wonder if he really knows what he is doing. However, if he had a few grease stains on his pants, had a dirty rag cloth, or even if he were rude, you would be more confident that he could do the job.

The same goes for a construction worker; if he comes into a meeting with a hard hat, you know he is the right guy for the job. He was absolutely right; we get blinded sometimes with what we think we should wear or say, that we forget to look at it from the other person's point of view.

My business was taking care of buildings and maintenance services. If I looked like an investment banker during the meeting, my client wouldn't take me too seriously, assuming I am new to the job or extremely expensive.

We developed this way of thinking when we are children in kindergarten, where we identify the people by their uniforms, saying, this is a fireman, a police officer, etc. So, this is your first impression.

Consider what impression you want to give to the other person and work towards it. Then, start the conversation where you think there is common ground and build towards that direction.

Remember, time is short, so use it to make a lasting impression when you get your shot.

CHAPTER 10
The Value of Giving Gifts

We usually give presents on occasions such as holidays, festivals, anniversaries, or as a gesture of goodwill. However, deciding what to give them can often be quite a dilemma. And often, we must make the decision quickly, here and NOW, so it's best to be prepared for making that choice in advance.

One should always acknowledge the gesture as it expresses how they value you and want to be remembered. It is insulting and ungrateful not to accept it. Sometimes we worry that we cannot return the favour in the same manner, or we might even consider that taking the present would mean you owe a favour in return.

Well, this could be true in certain situations. But in general, you should always accept a gift when presented to you.

While choosing a gift, you should determine whether it shows the actual meaning of why you would want to give it to them. If it is not clear, it is always advisable to write a letter along with the gift telling the recipient what they mean to you and why you thought of them in this manner. By doing so, the present becomes more even more valuable.

While giving a gift, one should not consider merely its monetary value; it means so much more for you to pick something uniquely valuable to them.

Take, for example, if someone has a hobby and collects coins. If you get them a new note or new coin from one of your trips, it may not have much value to you, but to the person who has the hobby, it means a whole lot as it shows that you thought of them when you were travelling. In turn, the person receiving it knows how much you value them and will appreciate it even more.

When giving a gift to a friend in a relationship, you should not upstage their spouse's gift. For example, if you consider buying jewellery for a friend, you cannot buy something more expensive or valuable than what she already has or what her spouse has bought her. It would make the spouse uncomfortable and even the person receiving it. In this case, your gift becomes more of a problem than a good gesture.

When you are unsure of what to give, it is always good to consider a few options, such as:

- Alcohol – spirits such as whiskey, tequila and so forth (either a bottle of what they regularly drink, if it is to a close friend) or something of a better calibre. If you give an expensive bottle of alcohol, it will never upstage a spouse like jewellery. Of course, people don't consider it like that, as it can be shared with everyone and even cherished and savoured for an even more special occasion.
- Wine – yes, I am aware wine is alcohol, but a bottle of wine is something nice to bring. When you go to someone's

house, it shows that you value their invitation and to thank them for their company.

- Sweets and Savory -- is also a good option when visiting someone's house, pastries, cakes, cheese platters, a plate of cold cuts, chocolates or sweets. Always get something of your choice on what you like in it, as it is a good conversation starter and something you can share with them on how special it is to you. (Keep in mind allergies/ religious restrictions.)

- For the house -- if you have been to their home in the past, and you know what they would cherish and enjoy, something like a vase, a centrepiece or a nice bowl is always a well-received present; just be alarmed, don't get pissed if you don't see it the next time you walk in.

- Money – for many festivities and holidays or even birthdays and weddings, money is always a good option when you want to give them a gift and are unsure what they will like. It is good to do it in style, though, so always have a card and write a note on what you recommend they should do with it and leave the rest up to them. If you don't have time to get a greeting card, a simple envelope will do, but be sure that it is placed in an envelope to give a more formal feel.

- Gift cards -- these are great gifts. When someone moves into a new house, it helps purchase furniture and appliances. However, gift cards for luxury stores are often a pure waste of money. Unless you know they shop there frequently, they may never use it.

Risky gifts

- Clothing -- unless you are very close to the person, it is almost certain that it either won't fit them, or they wouldn't like the style.
- Perfumes – everyone prefers a particular scent; so, the chances are that your gift will be re-gifted, which is not a great feeling; don't put yourself in that position.
- Jewellery – whether if it is imitation jewellery or authentic, it is very personal. It might not be something your friend would choose to wear. Buying them a beautiful necklace might seem nice, but if they don't ever wear it, it is kind of a waste for both individuals.

All gifts are extra special when wrapped. It creates an element of surprise that always adds value to the moment.

Remember, the value of the gift lies in it being an appropriate gift for the occasion and useful for the person, not merely for its value. And when you give a gift, don't do it to expect something in return. If you are giving something, it should be what you are comfortable giving and what you want to give. You, too, might have an unexpected gift coming from someone else altogether. The true feeling of happiness is when you give someone a present without expecting anything in return.

The **Manner** of giving is worth more than the gift.

CHAPTER 11
Save Your Stuff from Childhood

As we discussed in the earlier chapter, our childhood moulds us into the adult we are today. It includes all our influences from childhood, from the toys we played with to the cartoons, music, and the chips and chocolates we loved. As we grow older, we hold on to the memories that were our earliest joys. Unconsciously, we often make decisions NOW based on these childhood inspirations. For example, that toy rocketship launched a NASA scientist to even greater heights than his childhood dreams.

As adults, we get our inspiration from the influences we had in our childhood. I am a child from the '80s, and I grew up on monopoly, Teenage mutant ninja turtles and Scrooge McDuck. Today some of the most expensive art revolves around these characters. Kids who played with them have now grown into adults, and this is something they can relate to in their childhood. The same goes for antiques, as it has value based on what it meant for a whole generation.

Designers and artists prosper by creating art that speaks to our childhood experiences. If a child grew up wanting something he could not have or didn't have enough of, when he grows up, that will be the first thing he would like to achieve, whether it might be a journey's destination or something to purchase. And as we grow from our childhood, what we grew up with fades away to bring newer things to life, and our past desires become priceless nostalgia.

Growing up as a kid, we seldom see the value in these things. Take the time to go through your parent's attic or storage room and discover if some of your childhood memories are stored there. They could be quite valuable either monetarily or just as a loving reminder of precious times of your childhood. The things we were exposed to in our childhood have influenced us to become the people we are today. We only realise this as we grow older and value the things we have lost. As history repeats itself, take care of these things, as eventually, they will increase in value for you and the whole generation that grew up with the same items.

CHAPTER 12
How to Choose and Maintain a Diet

Of all the chapters, this one probably best epitomises the concept of making a decision NOW. When you are in the supermarket, your less-than-perfect instincts pick out the worst culprits for your health. The biggest offenders are snacks such as chocolates, chips, candies, as opposed to other organic and healthier snacks. Your diet should be what your body needs for growth and sustenance. Of course, we all slip now and then, but our eating habits should be for a healthy diet, not the other way around.

Usually, people start a diet when they want to lose weight and try a diet they have been told or read about. So, they begin the new diet without all the "goodies" from their old diet and think, "this sucks!" They miss the sugar, salt, candy, etc. and start to wonder if the sacrifice is absolutely necessary. But the real sacrifice is to your health if you don't maintain a healthy diet. Sticking to a diet mainly starts with portion control, meaning you can have a slice of pizza, but eating the whole pizza, shouldn't be an option.

It's like tapering off smoking, where you consciously make an effort day by day till you completely stop smoking. That's the same way you start a diet; you taper off the old one and make way for the new one.

If you work out regularly in the gym, your diet includes mainly protein to build muscle and less processed and saturated fats, as it isn't something that would give energy. And, it's important to have a diet that gives you enough nutrients; otherwise, it uses up the body's reserve, and you end up getting tired faster.

An excellent HEALTHY MEAL comes directly from the earth, as all living things do. Choose organic fruits and vegetables and opt for proteins not injected with hormones.

You can maintain your diet if you listen to what your body tells you and nurture it to reach the desired changes. It's like having a ginger shot; most find it very bitter and hard to drink. However, once you start making your own, you end up drinking a glass of it easily.

Many people think eating healthier is expensive since organic and natural foods are usually more expensive in supermarkets. Still, good quality fruits and vegetables and fewer meats will fill you up and give you the results you want with much less quantity than processed and junk food.

Many of you think your healthy goal is hard to achieve. However, it all starts with one step. You won't reach your end goal without taking a step in the right direction, so starting your diet is the first step, and not giving up is the second.

A diet is also helpful to understand how much you would spend on food a month. Whether you eat out at a restaurant or prepare your meals at home, a definite diet plan will significantly lower your food costs. Do the math, and you will see the difference.

There are so many ways to begin a diet. Ignore your inner excuses and educate yourself about which diet will be best for you and your mindset.

CHAPTER 13
Why Do Life Insurance?

Life insurance is the premium that one pays, monthly, quarterly, annually etc., as a policy to protect our loved ones in the event of our death. And life insurance can save you a lot of money if you plan it right and use it to the full extent possible. Unfortunately, it is perhaps one of the most procrastinated decisions people make. We have all seen the television commercials where the wife tells the husband she wants him to get a policy NOW and quit putting it off until "they can afford it".

Life insurance usually insures people's lives till the age of 60, sometimes 65, depending on the country or the region. Depending on the policy, you will usually pay a regular premium over 10 – 15 years, and it will insure your life until the policy's maturity date. There are policies for those older than 60, but they are usually limited to term policies designed to cover burial expenses.

A life insurance policy guarantees that in case of your loss of life, the people you leave behind will be the benefactors of the amount that you have insured your life for.

It is always good to insure your life for more than the debt you owe, so you don't leave behind anyone with that burden. If you don't owe any debts, then you leave your loved ones with money to spend however they choose.

If you survive the age of 60, make sure your policy that you have taken includes a payout either in a lump sum or as a pension, and be clear about how you want it to be dispersed in the end.

While taking a policy, it is important to consider an international policy. If you are based out of multiple cities, accessing the funds is easier and can be quickly transferred.

Many people forget to check the taxation policy. If the life insurance matures and the net amount will be taxed or not, a law applies in which if you take the policy from a non-taxation country, the net amount you received won't be taxed. So, it is possible; you just need to be smart enough to figure it out.

Also, taking an international policy provider helps if you have other banking tools, such as loans, mortgages, or finances.

Usually, when you take out a large loan, banks and other institutions always protect themselves and take a life policy on you which you pay for as part of your loan payment. When you pay off the loan, you cannot recover the amount you have paid for this insurance.

The best way to negotiate it is to let the bank give you a breakdown of your premium. Then you ask them if you can put the bank as a benefactor on your insurance policy where the amount of your insurance should cover the liability. In that case, the bank will be more than happy to do so as they are protected. So, now you continue paying your existing life insurance policy instead of wasting money on insuring the loan/liability separately.

I suggest always using the larger international firms like ZURICH or Generali, simply because they are the most used in the banking field, and everyone more readily accepts them instead of your local insurance provider.

Lastly, a life insurance policy is considered a basic form of savings account. The interest yield is extremely low, but the peace of mind it brings your dependents is high.

CHAPTER 14
What to Ask When Buying a Business

In life, sometimes, you will have an opportunity to buy a business, partner with one, or even start your own business. However, this is one of those major life decisions where you should not leap into it until you have thoroughly investigated it. In this case, the NOW of when you make that decision must be carefully planned.

When deciding to buy a business or take over a business, people tend to be confused about what they should consider before buying it. Here are a few pointers on what you should ask and why it's essential to know the answers.

What do you have in inventory?

The type, quantity (weight) or volume of stock, units, etc., gives you an estimate of what can be sold, so this would tell you how much of stock you can turn around or sell before reordering or manufacturing, depending on the business.
- What the inventory includes
   - The number of items you have completed that just need to be sold
   - The number of items that go hand in hand in assembling or are involved in the process to get a finished product
      - The number of items that are fit to use

- Output capacity
  - ° The current output of the business, whether it may be in manufacturing or service
  - ° Capable output in full capacity/ full engagement of resources
- Machinery - if in manufacturing
  - ° When it was acquired, if it has any warranty, and what is the maintenance cost associated with it, along with the list of contacts that one would need in case of a breakdown or emergency occurs
  - ° How it has been treated on the books if the asset has been depreciated correctly.
  - ° How much value does the machinery still hold?
  - ° Compare it with the price of buying a used machine, and whether the value of the machine is lower than buying a used machine.

Where is the location of the business?

Is the land included in the sale or lease (if leased, what is the period)?

What is the amount that is paid? You need to know this, so you can treat the expense correctly and know how much the overhead is and when the last payments were made. So, it's important to have the receipts.

If it's a bought piece of land:
- The documents for the transfer must be proper and updated in the records during the transfer

- Is the amount amortised over a period of time?
- What is the current market value? Compare it with the most similar piece of land and permit use that has sold recently; word of mouth is not enough proof.
- Compare it with the land's original value and what it is today to understand whether it has reached its maximum value or has room to increase the value.
- Real estate can be one of the most significant assets on the books for some businesses.

If it is a leased property:

- How long is the lease for, and when will it expire? Keep in mind; you must negotiate the rate at the end of the term. Determine if the landlord will permit the rent to stay the same, or if you want it lower, you have to negotiate it with the landlord and have it in writing to be protected.
- Is the lease they are currently paying on par with the current market price? (compare a similar place in the same are on what it rents for, your local lands department will be useful to understand the statistics.)
- What the lease covers:
  - Parking provisions
  - Location access
  - How many deposits, values, dates, and the receipts
  - Number of keys and penalties for lost keys, depending on the landlord
  - The asset list on what must be returned and what belongs to the building, examples: air conditioners, furniture, exhausts, fixtures, etc.
  - Payment schedule, last payments made, and a statement from the landlord that all dues are up to date.

What is the all-inclusive price of the business?

We do this to understand how much this business will cost us with everything taken into consideration. This is important for us to know as the parties selling the business tend to be in a position where they want to make the most profit and often don't mention liabilities that are not obvious.

How much is the current revenue from ongoing projects and in hand?

This helps understand how the business is currently performing. Before any new owner comes and makes their changes, this is the current revenue expected to come into the business, without any changes by the new owner.

What are the prospective orders in the pipeline?

As the word pipeline suggests, this is the estimated future sales based on past sales and projections by the current sales team. The hit rate is the conversion of the number of attempts in trying to close a sale. When analysing a pipeline, it is safe to assume a certain percentage of what will materialise, depending on the business. It varies if you are selling a service or a product and whether it is unique or in a competitive space. So, pipelines are essential to know what we can target, but a very low conversion percentage should be given. When one acquires the business, it is like changing captains in a football match; the game will be played differently. So, it is important to assume the worst as we won't be able to accurately estimate how the market will behave.

Who are the primary clients?

You need to gauge whether the current client roster adequately supports the business and if their relationship will continue after the sale or transfer. In addition, it's important to know if the company's sustainability is based on a few major clients or spread across numerous clients to understand if the loss of any of the big clients would adversely affect the business.

What are the outstanding accounts payable?

Payables are the amounts that you have to pay when you take over the business, including any outstanding cheques the company has given, money owed to suppliers, or even the dues that are to be paid to government bodies and so forth. Keeping the payables under control is very important as it affects its health, financially and legally. This is why it's vital to keep your books current and accurate. Always compare the previous year's payables from an audited balance sheet to the current year to have an idea about the truth. Here are a few general practices one must adhere to when dealing with liabilities:

- Determine the outstanding liabilities owed by the business. These need to be paid by the seller before the sale's closing unless otherwise agreed to by you. You should receive a "no due" certificate at the closing, indicating what has been paid.
- All liabilities which remain need to be documented in the sale agreement.

What are the business's assets?

It is essential to know how the assets are classified under the business and what they are. Here are a few points that one must consider regarding assets:

- If they still hold value at the time of the sale, compare with current prices in the market, and see if it has been amortised and depreciated over time
- If it is to bring in consistent revenue
- If it is to be sold, how much money would it bring
- The ownership titles in all the assets to be clear and documented

Audited financials are essential, preferably from a reputed auditing firm in your area, so you understand that the owner hasn't misappropriated the number and the audit firm stands by it. One can learn how much the company has grown in the years, as you can compare the revenue/profits and losses/withdrawals and overall performance of the company,

If you don't know how to read an audited financial and what it tells you, you should go to an expert and get some feedback to understand if it's a company you want to buy.

Reason for selling

You want to understand if the business is a liability to the owner and if the current owner doesn't want to hold on to it for a specific purpose. People don't let go of their golden goose that easily.

Many owners want their business to continue, but they are no longer fit to run it because of age or stress. They may also want to protect the current employees from losing their jobs. Whichever the reason it may be, it is important to know and understand the truth behind the sale. No hidden surprises!!!

CHAPTER 15
Travel Tips When Flying

We all travel through airports, and certain busy and popular airports, have over a million people going in and out of the airport daily. You have made several decisions already, including when to fly, which airline and what to pack for the trip.

Here is a checklist of some essential travel tips one should keep in mind:

1. When travelling, always wear pants, preferably sweatpants, that hold you tight to the ankle, and the sweatpants work as a bubble effect, protecting your legs and especially your ankles. Also, wearing sweatpants means not wearing a belt to avoid that hassle regarding the security check.

2. Always when you're packing your hand carry, keep your phone chargers in your side pockets so that you can charge your phone either on the flight or at the airport.

3. Your laptop should be the last thing you pack, as it would be the first thing you have to take out when you need to scan your hand carry.

4. Try to avoid carrying any form of liquids or gels. If necessary, bring them in a separate sandwich plastic bag.

5. The airports do their part in cleaning and disinfecting the facility. However, airports can be a honey trap for spreading infection and diseases irrespective of their excellent service. Therefore, one must always be careful when travelling through the airport.

6. Always wear socks and shoes. When you go into the airport, the airport houses millions of travellers, wearing sandals/flip-flops is a no-no regarding hygiene. Also, the chemicals used for cleaning the airports are much stronger than generic cleaning products and can cause irritations to bare feet. So, shoes are the only way to go.

7. Also, we know travellers sometimes like to take their shoes off during the flight, so having a pair of socks on is still a layer of protection. Keep in mind, the aircraft cannot be disinfected as much as the floor in an airport. So, it's advisable to never take your socks out during the flight, and it's also discomforting to your fellow passengers.

8. When you clear immigration, always check if your passport is stamped with the correct date. Most countries still have immigration control done by an actual person, and they can make an error. You need to check it, as there can be confusion upon arrival at one's port of destination. You would be detained until they verify the actual date, which would mean contacting the port of departure and confirming the details.

9. Before travelling to the airport, cut your fingernails and toenails. While travelling, they can collect a lot of dirt and bacteria and give you a fungal infection. Trim those critters.

10. Before boarding the flight, always buy a medium to a large water bottle, depending on the flight. Although the airline does provide water, certain carriers have the policy to start service only once take off. If it is a full flight, one can experience delays in being served. Therefore, having your own reserve is important.

11. Try to avoid taking any medication while travelling. For example, some travellers consume sleeping pills for long flights. However, it is not advisable, as when we are at that altitude, our body reacts very differently to the air pressure than on the ground.

12. Also, some people enjoy drinking on the plane. The same internal pressure makes you feel drunk faster, but not because your blood alcohol content is higher at elevation. Less oxygen is available to your brain at altitude, and our bodies are simultaneously attempting to acclimate to lower oxygen levels. Hence, your body reacts differently; taking medication is not advisable.

13. Fun Fact: for men, facial hair tends to grow faster after a flight. Studies show that a significant increase in internal pressure leads to accelerated growth of hair. So, be sure not to forget the essentials.

14. Last but not least, carry headphones. A good pair of headphones/earphones helps you be in your zone and avoid external noise. It also helps avoid conversations, even if you have nothing to listen to; popping them on would make people think you are listening and leave you alone.

This list should be a good framework for your pre-flight plans in the future. NOW is the time for you to create your own so you will be prepared for your next flight. Write it down and keep it where you will see it easily before your trip. Safe travels!

CHAPTER 16
Your Credit Card Strategy

Credit cards can be a blessing or a curse, depending on how you use them. There are so many decisions to make regarding them, but if you don't read anything else on this page, read this: pay your monthly balance in full NOW.

A credit card is a financial instrument provided to you based on your income, credit history or deposits that you have with the bank. Traditionally, you have 30-45 days to pay the amount charged back to the bank, interest-free. After that time and you haven't paid the whole amount, interest is calculated on your outstanding balance after your minimum payment and compounded accordingly. When I say compound, I mean if you have $30,000 due and pay $300 with an interest rate of 4%, the amount due is $30,888 on your next statement. If you continue to only pay the minimum payment on the following month, the same is true. Therefore, more interest will accrue via compounding.

This can get into a vicious cycle, and you, in turn, ending up paying large amounts of interest, and failing to do so, hurts your credit rating and can create immense legal situations. It is not a position you want to be in.

Credit cards, if planned well, can be beneficial, and you can save a lot of money. Here are a few things to consider and to keep always in mind:

1. This is worth repeating. First and foremost, pay your balance in full and don't let the bank earn interest.
2. Set up your payment date a week after you get paid or generally earn money, so you settle that first before anything else.
3. If you travel a lot, get a credit card with your airline of choice. You will earn miles when you spend, which in turn you can use to either buy tickets or upgrades on your airline ticket. Additionally, a credit card with your favourable hotel partner also gives you the same perks. Today hotels want to beat third-party booking websites. So, the privileges for hotel members at times supersede the value and cost of the booking websites.
4. Put all your payments you would typically pay cash for on your card. If you don't travel much and want to save money, a cashback card is what you are looking for. You must keep in mind that only payments of your outstanding balance will earn cash back for the next cycle and simply credit back to your credit card. It isn't a cash earner; a cashback card for grocery shopping is just for convenience.
5. Don't have a high limit; credit bureaus don't calculate your debt on how many cards you have but on your overall amount exposure. If you have 100,000 on one credit card or 25,000 on four credit cards, they will be looked at the same way irrespective of how much is outstanding and how much credit is used.

6. If you are a business owner, determine which card you want to use to make purchases and segregate that card mainly for business purposes. You earn miles/points and enjoy the privileges accordingly. There isn't anything criminal or illegal about what you are doing; it's a win-win situation.

7. Be disciplined, use your card specifically for the purpose you have it, and try to avoid using it for any other purpose that would only complicate your life mentally.

8. Also, while travelling to a foreign place you go to constantly, use a card with that currency, so you avoid paying for foreign exchange. If you don't travel to the same place very frequently and go to different countries, then have a separate card for travel purposes.

9. Set up direct deposits for your rent, any monthly instalments, insurance payments and so forth to use under your credit card that you can earn points on. This way, you can earn points when technically you have just paid an expense and not bought anything with it. Be smart and make the most of your payments.

I can't stress this enough though, don't let your balances cumulate and pay them immediately. Spend only the money you can afford. Don't overspend thinking you are earning miles/ points on it. Treat it like a debit card with privileges, and that has given you a 30-day interest-free period. Spend wisely.

CHAPTER 17
Gold Rules!

Historically gold is considered the most precious metal and is even more valuable than diamonds. The earliest civilisations traded with gold coins, and many still do. The whole fascination with gold began when most countries, including America, based their currencies on the amount of gold reserves they would have. However, in the 70's America no longer tied its currency to the gold standard.

Gold still held its value because of its demand and because it will always be accepted as currency. Many people want to keep some of their money in gold. It is less convenient than currency in taking it and spending it immediately, as one would need to sell it and then get their money. Also, the rate at which gold fluctuates is not as volatile as the currencies.

In Asia, acquiring gold is very popular with most people who can afford to do so, as there is always value and stability with gold compared to most assets. In addition, it is malleable; you can wear it as jewellery and ornaments or save it as gold bars. Diamonds don't have this ability. Also, assessing a diamond's value gets tricky as the larger the diamond, the harder to liquidate, depending on the price and situation of the market.

Gold's malleability quality holds in this account. Gold testing also gives gold a more accurate denominator than diamonds, where if someone isn't as knowledgeable as a jeweller, they can be taken for a ride. On the other hand, gold is used in manufacturing, creating chips in computers, electronics, medical uses, aerospace uses, etc. So, the demand always stays high as it is needed in various industries apart from popular jewellery. This demand helps in holding its price and future demand as well.

Whenever you save money, keep a certain amount in gold. Historically, gold is stable and increases in value over time, unlike cash, which would decrease with inflation if stored the same way or wouldn't make money for you by just holding it, as gold does. So, if you can afford it, buy some gold NOW. Gold Rules!!

CHAPTER 18
Are You Going to Change the World?

We all are here to change the world. Most of us feel insignificant at one time or the other in life and think that we don't make a difference. And that if we weren't present, the world would still move on, and no one would miss you. This is true!

The world moves on irrespective of you or any individual. Whether there are natural disasters or terrorist attacks, people still must live and get on with their lives as long as they are alive. This is the spirit of life. The decisions you make today, NOW, may impact yourself, your family and, indeed, the rest of the world.

When it came to recycling, initially, I thought, *Why should I be the one to do it? What would my little effort amount to in the scheme of things?* I can let others do it because one less person won't matter. But over time, if you think like that, you will always be insignificant. One person often brings about a change in the world, but if more people follow, then that change becomes much more significant.

Often, a religion was started by a single prophet. Imagine if they felt the same insignificance you have felt; the faith would have never reached the masses.

You must realise one essential thing. Whichever part of life you are in right now, whether a teenager, or in your 20's or 30's, or older, time will march on, with or without you. In time, you will grow older and have less energy and resources to meet your journey's goals.

So, remember that you are very significant and press forward full-speed on your journey now, or you will regret it when you grow older. However, don't forget that it takes time and patience to achieve that goal. So, remember the mango tree; time makes the fruit sweet. Likewise, nobody is born a leader; leaders grow just like fruit on a tree. So don't take the risk of not thinking that you can be the catalyst for change.

Don't battle the voice in your head; it is your voice of understanding. Listen to it; it goes away when your mind is occupied with your daily life, so when it comes, listen to it. It is louder when you are younger cause all the information is new, and your mind is absorbing everything like a sponge.

So, when the voice gets quieter and comes less often, it's a sign of maturity and your mind is occupied with what you already know. This means you must listen even more intently.

Don't be afraid of change; change is inevitable. Instead, embrace it and try to make it a change for the better. A better you and a better world for us to live in.

And always remember what Socrates said:

"True knowledge exists in knowing that you know nothing."

Be humble, be truthful to yourself and always respect your roots and where you come from, and the world will be your oyster and yours for the taking.

Message from the Author

Thank you for taking the time to read my book. If I imparted some knowledge and helped you benefit in looking at life differently, I have achieved the purpose of my book. I have always been in a hurry in going through life and trying to achieve my goals and dreams. I was a firm believer in NOW, but as I have grown older, I realise that NOW needs to be paired with careful decision making. Being able to share my experiences to help others avoid situations I have faced is my goal. We have one life; make it count. There isn't a reset button, and if you feel you haven't made the most of it, that's alright; you still have time to start.

Everything in life has an expiry date, the milk in your fridge, the fruits on the tree, and there is a limited time to consume it. Also, consider that many people who come into your life are here for a short time. So, cherish those moments, and once it's over, don't trouble yourself on why it is over. Just know that they were supposed to be there in your life. Their purpose of coming into your life was to either teach you a skill, impart knowledge, or simply share and learn an experience together. So, be thankful for the good and the bad; this is how life teaches you lessons.

If you find yourself in a difficult situation and asking the question, "Why is this happening to me?" understand it is the choices you have made in life that have led you to this point. Know there is a cost associated with it which you must bear or go through. This time will pass, be strong, keep your head high, and do what it takes to get you back. The answer always lies within YOU. I leave you with this quote from His Holiness The Dalai Lama:

"If you wish to experience peace, provide peace for another."

Sharath Shanth with Tenzin Gyatso,
His Holiness, the 14th Dalai Lama

Acknowledgements

I want to especially thank my parents for providing such a nurturing home for me to become the man I have become today and my little sister, whom I love very much.

And to all the people who I have met along my journey who have given me love and knowledge, I am forever grateful for allowing me to be part of your journey. Thank you for being YOU.

I send a special shout out to my Harvard alumni, OPM51.

I hope my book enlightens you, guides you, and will help you along your journey through life.